PRIVATE PARTIES

Allan Havis

Broadway Play Publishing Inc
224 E 62nd St, NY, NY 10065
www.broadwayplaypub.com
info@broadwayplaypub.com

PRIVATE PARTIES
©2010 by Allan Havis

First printing: June 2010
I S B N: 978-0-88145-455-0

Book design: Marie Donovan
Typography/page layout: Adobe InDesign
Typeface: Palatino Linotype
Printed and bound in the U S A

PRIVATE PARTIES was first produced by Sixth@Penn (Artistic Producing Director, Dale Morris). The cast and creative contributors were:

LETI	Julia Fulton
PEARL	Kristie Sessions
Director	Kirsten Brandt
Assistant director	Robin Christ
Stage manager	Madeline Cohen
Lighting & set design	Rich Covert
Costume ddesign	Mary Larson

CHARACTERS & SETTING

LETI, *late thirties/early forties attractive, edgy woman who lacks a permanent address, gainful employment, and a circle of friends or relatives. She has a habit of impulsive arguing and confiding, too often in the same breath. The latest love of her life is an old Ford Mustang which she is determined to sell to the truest buyer in California. She's an optimist, and prefers to kiss rather than punch. Cabo is a geographical goal, by detour through Tijuana and sleepy Rosarito—along Mexico's Baja penisula.*

PEARL, *mid to late twenties, energetic, alert, as good looking as LETI, presently living in Los Angeles. Her knowledge of cars often impresses others, particularly car guys. There is something about her which defies analysis, but suffice it to say that she's rapidly approaching her very long awaited "defining moment". Freedom is a missing component in her life, yet she pushes herself to find the right opportunity to become utterly new to herself. LETI fascinates her; her excesses do not repel, they inspire.*

Seven scenes set in La Jolla, California & Rosarito Beach, Mexico.

Time is the present; present is the time.

in memory of a young student playwright Eric Bowling

Scene One

(LETI's sidewalk in in front of her address in La Jolla, California. She's thinking about smoking the cigarette in her hand. PEARL approaches from the nearby mailbox.)

LETI: Pearl?

PEARL: Yeah.

LETI: White Pearl??

PEARL: That's right.

LETI: Pearly white Pearl? You said you had red hair.

PEARL: When the sun's out. But I don't dye my hair. *(Silence)* The address was wrong.

LETI: No.

PEARL: No?

LETI: No. You wrote it down wrong.

PEARL: I guess so.

LETI: You don't look that stupid.

PEARL: I was off by one crappy number. *(Pause)* Is this your home?

LETI: No. I'm only staying for a few days. You know how it is.

PEARL: What?

LETI: Staying a day or two as a house guest. You become a goddamn nuisance.

PEARL: Yeah.

LETI: You're late.

PEARL: Am I?

LETI: An hour at least.

PEARL: Can't be an hour.

LETI: Look at your watch.

(PEARL *does*.)

LETI: Am I shitting you?

PEARL: I tried to phone, but your line was busy.

LETI: It was off the hook.

PEARL: I guess the car is sold?

LETI: Would it break your heart?

PEARL: I drove three hours.

LETI: A cop put down a hundred to hold it...but that wouldn't work.

PEARL: Yeah, ahuh.

LETI: Circumstances prevail.

PEARL: The cop low-balled you?

LETI: You know how cops are. The chubby ones with bushy moustaches and piggly warts.

PEARL: He didn't want the car?

LETI: No, he wanted the goddamn car.

PEARL: Oh.

LETI: But his focus was on the wrong chasse. Maybe it was the way I was dressed. I try to be sensible. Otherwise I get in trouble. I've Byzantine dreams.

PEARL: Cool.

LETI: I chased him away. Didn't want his money. (*Pause*) I dreamt that I would die inside this Mustang. Hellish nightmare. Flying off a bridge over the Pacific.

Couldn't roll down the windows. Green water filling my lungs. Knowing this was my assigned page. Dying alone. End of a mystery.

PEARL: Dying is a mystery.

LETI: Right. I took this as a sign of punishment from above. That's how Stephen King got hit by that car in Maine. He had a tax to pay. You write horror, horror writes you back. I'm not saying that my hang up is yours. But my shadow sticks close to me. And there's comfort to that.

PEARL: I guess I should go.

LETI: I had a life before I fell into free-fall. Can't settle in California.

PEARL: Roots take time.

LETI: You're right. Don't go, Pearl. *(Pause)* You want this car badly, don't you?

PEARL: Yeah.

LETI: Yeah?

PEARL: Yeah. I like the car, yeah. My boyfriend got me started on Ford classics. T-birds, Cougars, the works. Pure Detroit metal wrapped and slapped. Mustang's a mythic star.

LETI: A classy star which aged beautifully. *(Sings)*
Pony car, pony car.
Won't you be my pony car?
Don't say no, here we go,
Ride across the plain *(She hums a few more bars)*

PEARL: Nothing's cooler than an early year Mustang.

LETI: What does your boyfriend drive?

PEARL: Nothing.

LETI: Oh?

PEARL: Not even a bicycle. D M V revoked his license. He flunked traffic school. Three D W Is and they crucify you and your first born.

LETI: Jail time?

PEARL: Six months.

LETI: He got off light.

PEARL: Nearly broke up his band.

LETI: What's the band?

PEARL: Pissin' In The Wind. Bluegrass with...

LETI: A twist of Lyle Lovett?

PEARL: No, that jerk called Moby.

LETI: How do they sound?

PEARL: Like white trash pissin' in the wind. *(Pause)* Can I test drive it, Leti?

LETI: Bring cash?

(PEARL *nods her head.*)

LETI: You're serious.

PEARL: About a lot of things.

LETI: Let's truck. You're about ten years my junior.

PEARL: Yeah

LETI: I can guess your weight too.

PEARL:

You and my boyfriend.

LETI: Don't get pissed.

PEARL: I'm not pissed. I like you. You're weird. *(Pause)* isten, I'm buying the car, that's a fact.

LETI: You just have that certain feeling.

PEARL: It looks O K from here. I go on hunches.

LETI: The car's got a soul of its own, I swear.

PEARL: Don't see that many ads like yours.

LETI: A fading muscle car deserves respect.

PEARL: Pure Ford genius.

LETI: Lithe and agile. Radio full blast. The car that America made great.

PEARL: Just a short test ride. Up the freeway and down the coast.

LETI: Sure thing! Listen sweetie...I can't find the keys.

PEARL: What?

LETI: There's another set inside the glove compartment.

PEARL: Car's locked?

LETI: More or less. *(Looking across the street)* Beautiful bitchin' car. We'll get the keys, honey.

PEARL: Leti...

LETI: My auto ambivalence acting up on me... *(Pause)* What happened to your face?

PEARL: *(Adjusting her sunglasses)* Just a bruise.

LETI: Some fucked up guy in an amateur band?

PEARL: Skip it.

LETI: I'd report the asshole at once.

PEARL: I did.

LETI: Boys and their boundary issues.

PEARL: Past history now.

LETI: Did you hear that the "N R A" Senator from Texas was shot inside a carwash?

PEARL: Today?

LETI: A set-up. No witnesses. The killer got away. Probably was his girlie intern from Corpus Christi. What's Charlton Heston going to say?

PEARL: Hell's Bells! Doesn't he have Alzheimer's?

LETI: Carwashes used to be very safe.

PEARL: Except for hydrochondriacs.

LETI: You mean hydrophobics?

PEARL: Hydroponics. Whatever.

LETI: Fact is, he wasn't a real friend of the N R A since he pushed trigger locks whenever he left the state. Texas is so fucking violent.

PEARL: Then again, there's Gary Condit from Modesto. He killed Chandra Levy.

LETI: You're so right, girl! *(Pause)* I'll probably get very upset after this Mustang drives away.

PEARL: So you said over the phone.

LETI: We need precious toys. Or a cherished house pet. The chestnut sweetness of a retriever. Lovely dog hairs everywhere. On the carpet, black dresses and the bed. Hugging an abandoned one from the pound makes me cry.

PEARL: That's so true.

LETI: I'm moving to Mexico. Had a fantastic dream about Cabo San Lucas.

PEARL: Cool. I've been there.

LETI: Selling everything I own.

PEARL: I did that a couple of years ago.

LETI: Good feeling.

PEARL: Lighter than a feather.

LETI: Going to design my own amnesia. A step toward absolute freedom.

PEARL: Money is freedom. That's my dad talking. *(Pause)* Thought about buying the new Mustang GT with the single-cam V8, 16 valves, duel exhaust.

LETI: Single-cam?

PEARL: Ahuh.

LETI: If the vibe is sweet, I don't sweat what's under the hood.

PEARL: I took a course through college extension.

LETI: Did you get your hands dirty?

PEARL: Never trust a mechanic with a hangdog smile sucking on a lollypop.

LETI: I like to hang a small rabbit's foot or a dream catcher under the mirror.

PEARL: How much will you take for it?

LETI: Didn't I say over the phone? If I really like you, three grand.

PEARL: Do you?

LETI: Better than blue book.

PEARL: Three grand?

LETI: I paid double that and rebuilt the engine.

PEARL: Mileage?

LETI: Odometer's busted. But I've got all the service records. Got to be under a hundred thousand.

PEARL: Three grand?

LETI: Look at the body. Not an ounce of rust. Pretty flashy for a '67.

PEARL: Obviously, it's had a paint job or two.

LETI: Who hasn't?

PEARL: My dad used to drive a Mustang. And he handled them like children. *(Pause)* You're going to use the coat hanger to get in?

LETI: Usually works.

PEARL: I hate when that happens.

LETI: I got a zillion coat hangers.

PEARL: Want me to do it?

LETI: No, I got this down pat.

PEARL: Got the proper title?

LETI: Of course.

PEARL

'Cause I drove two and a half hours in killer traffic.

LETI: Relax. My life is tied up with this sweet car.

PEARL: Yeah, I understand.

LETI: No you don't. I gave birth inside this Mustang.

PEARL: Really?

LETI: Couple of years ago. Right after Sinatra died.

PEARL: You're shittin' me.

LETI: Sinatra's not your guy, I can tell. You go for Sting or Harry Connick, right? Barry Manilow? I was late in my third trimester. I had some prescription painkillers and pulled myself down along the seat.

PEARL: Lamaze?

LETI:Lamaze my ass. A Christian SuperAgency came aboard. Jesus Family Values something or other. My blue haired aunt got involved. Thinks she's D A R. Those things matter to her. *(Pause)* A few pounds underweight.

PEARL: Boy or girl?

LETI: Auntie Clara gave her a temp name. Sounded like Mayflower. That's like having a freaking boat for a baby. Lost her to adoption services.

PEARL: That's kind of sad, Leti.

LETI: Yeah. *(She employs the coat hanger in the manner of a "fishing arm" to hook the inside door lock.)* Whenever I slip in without a key, it's good to think about historic things like orgasms and the acquisition of fine jewelery.

PEARL: *(Attention on car lock)* For sure.

LETI: Yeah, just another flick of the wrist...

PEARL: I really really want this car, Leti.

LETI: Bingo! *(Successful in opening car door)* In time, she will return your affection beyond your dreams. And your happiness will lift my happiness. *(Pause)* Were you ever pregnant?

PEARL: Why do you ask?

LETI: Cause I like to know what I already know.

PEARL: I don't think you need to know.

LETI: Maybe. We've a few items in common.

PEARL: Most women do.

LETI: And you had an abortion.

PEARL: Excuse me?

LETI: Within the last two years.

PEARL: And if I did?

LETI: I doubt no one knows.

PEARL: My father knows.

LETI: At least he was compassionate.

PEARL: He was. *(Pause)* I think it's time for a test drive.

LETI: Yeah. *(Pause)* Can I see your license?

PEARL: *(Retrieving from her purse)* Just a sec.

LETI: Insurance says you got to do that, otherwise...not that I don't trust you. Want me to come with you?

PEARL: *(Hands over license)* That goes without saying...

LETI: I 'll just make you really nervous. That's O K. Feel the car alone. You don't need to crash into a eucalyptus all because of me.

PEARL: I'll be back in five minutes.

LETI: I'll just hold on to your license, O K? Next month's your birthday. Only twenty-eight.

(PEARL *nods in agreement*)

LETI: There's enough gas in the car to hit the freeway. Feel the pick up at eighty. And if a cop comes, tell him the speedometer's busted and I have your I D.

PEARL: My dad's a cop.

LETI: Then absolutely no harm shall come to you. Amen.

(*End of scene*)

Scene Two

(*An hour later*)

PEARL: I love the car, Leti.

LETI: Ahuh.

PEARL: I really love the car.

LETI: Took you a fine freaking hour to figure that out?

PEARL: Time flew.

LETI: Where did you go, my dear?

PEARL: Here and there. Ran out of gas. Had to keep driving.

LETI: Yeah.

PEARL: I used to live not far from here. So I cruised around with the radio on.

LETI: Hope you didn't change the stations. I got them set just right.

PEARL: Doesn't matter.

LETI: You'll like my stations, honey.

PEARL: We'll see. Any budge on the price?

LETI: I gave you my best price.

PEARL: Three grand?

LETI: What do you want me to do, wrap it in a pink bow? *(Pause)* So where are we?

PEARL: I've cash.

LETI: Count it out please.

PEARL: *(Hands a wad of cash)* All hundreds. Nice, crisp and clean. Straight from the bank.

LETI: Not taking it to a mechanic?

PEARL: The car sounds and handles fine.

LETI: O K.

PEARL: O K.

LETI: Okey dokey. *(Pause)* I thought you might steal the Mustang.

PEARL: I don't steal.

LETI: We all steal sometimes. *(Counting cash)* I'd have gone to the cops. I'm not afraid of cops. I can charm a cop. My father wanted to be a cop.

PEARL: That right?

LETI: All his friends were cops or they looked like very glazed donuts. *(Putting cash in her pocket)* This counts O K, Pearl.

PEARL: I tried to get into the trunk. *(Next two lines overlap)* But this key doesn't work.

LETI: Sometimes the lock sticks. All you got to do is stop at a gas station or a 7/11. They'll fix it.

PEARL: Don't you have a trunk key?

LETI: It's lost in the crease of the rear seat. No big deal. It'll turn up after your first full car wash.

PEARL: I really should have a look inside.

LETI: I've got the title in my purse. *(Fishing it out)* It's got a coffee stain. Demons have chased away my angels. You know what I mean?

PEARL: Angels never really leave you.

LETI: *(Smiling)* Here's the title. And bill of sale. How do you spell your name?

PEARL: Like an ocean pearl. Last name Campbell.

LETI: Like the soup can?

PEARL: Like the soup can.

LETI: I wish you a lot of luck with this baby blue beauty, Pearl Campbell.

PEARL: Thank you.

LETI: I wish myself luck too.

PEARL: All one can hope for.

LETI: Yeah, girl. That's all one can hope for.

PEARL: Anything you need to get from the car?

LETI: If you find any tapes in the glove compartment, they're yours. Even Tom Petty. I give up everything. Such things you will inherit from me. I'm never going back. Don't miss my family. California's only going to bring me an early death. *(Pause)* And, for Godsake, please drive safe. Don't see any cute angels on duty today.

(End of scene)

Scene Three

(The next day. PEARL *has sounded the car horn for several seconds.* LETI *approaches slowly, smoking a cigarette with a bandaged hand.)*

LETI: I thought it was you.

PEARL: It's me all right.

LETI: Honking like that will only piss off the neighbors.

PEARL: You wouldn't answer at the door.

LETI: I was in the shower.

PEARL: Don't give a shit.

LETI: What a hot day. It's going to broil! *(Pause)* Better check the oil and water.

PEARL: Fuck the oil and water.

LETI: You're angry at me.

PEARL: Ahuh.

LETI: You've been in my thoughts, Pearl.

PEARL: Yeah.

LETI: You're really angry.

PEARL: Bet you dear ass I am.

LETI: It's understandable.

PEARL: Do I look like some frickin' idiot?

LETI: Not at all.

PEARL: Then are you some kind of frickin' idiot?

LETI: I feel like one, yeah. *(Pause)* Why don't we go out for some lunch?

PEARL: I didn't come for lunch.

LETI: We got to do something about your anorexic behavior.

PEARL: I'm not anorexic, Missy.

LETI: Starvation will take years off your love life.

PEARL: I opened the trunk.

LETI: When?

PEARL: This morning.

LETI: You found the key under the floor mat?

(PEARL *nods.*)

LETI: And you thought it was a Halloween prank?

PEARL: We're months past Halloween.

LETI: Can I explain?

PEARL: Ahuh.

LETI: The short version, or the longer one?

PEARL: The truth, any which way.

LETI: O K.

PEARL: O K.

LETI: O K.

PEARL: There's nearly seventy thousand in the trunk

LETI: Money is freedom, Pearl. Or is that your dad talking?

PEARL: I don't want it.

LETI: Most people would.

PEARL: Quit bullshitting me.

LETI: Sorry. I'm not bullshitting you.

PEARL: You're a murderer.

LETI: Don't presume things.

PEARL: Who's body is that?

LETI: It's Ralph.

PEARL: Ralph who?

LETI: Ralph Kroeger.

PEARL: Who the hell's Ralph Kroeger?

LETI: Just some asshole.

PEARL: Who is he Leti?

LETI: My ex-boyfriend.

PEARL: You killed him.

LETI: No. I swear to you. It was his mother.

PEARL: His mother?

LETI: This Neanderthal woman, that's right.

PEARL: You're lying.

LETI: I don't lie about death.

PEARL: You're a nut case, Leti.

LETI: And you're not?

PEARL: Why risk bringing me into this?

LETI: The color of your hair. *(Pause)* I like your hair.

PEARL: You're worse than insane.

LETI: Only in brief, elliptical moments. Otherwise, I'm quite stable.

PEARL: Why choose me?

LETI: You chose the ad.

PEARL: But you did choose me.

LETI: I should ask you the same question. *(Pause)* I had a dream about you months ago. What do you make of that?

PEARL: Don't say anything more.

LETI: It was the sweetest dream all year. We sat inside a smoke filled bistro. Another country, Brazil. The waiters all looked like old dates, deadbeats, and rats. You know the look. It was a dream which deeply linked us. I guessed all answers to your future. We share a darling fate. *(Pause)* That's not my house. It's his mother's. And she's sleeping in the next room from my bedroom. This woman could give head to a rhino. You know what I mean?

PEARL: No.

LETI: She's hard and cruel, Pearl.

PEARL: Does she suspect anything?

LETI: I really don't know. I drop hints, but the bitch misses the barn door. I want her to know. I want to see the morbid expression on her pockmarked face. She thinks he's on a fishing trip with the boys. The bastard never went fishing in his entire life. She never grew to like me, told me that last Thanksgiving. Why? Because I didn't baste enough. Even Wolfgang Puck couldn't baste this bird enough. Too dry to eat, she screamed. Sixteen pounds of dead fowl. She took the roasting pan out to the driveway and backed her boxy Volvo right over it.

PEARL: That explains nothing.

LETI: Nobody ate that night.

PEARL: She must really hate you.

LETI: I don't blame her.

PEARL: She'll catch you.

LETI: Only if I let her. She's not stupid. This is making you uncomfortable.

PEARL: I am uncomfortable.

LETI: How can I make you feel better? *(Pause)* Maybe I can do you a favor? *(Pause)* I see a fat question mark on your brow.

PEARL: Did you kill him? Simple yes or no.

LETI: Would you believe it was a coronary?

PEARL: No.

LETI: That's what an autopsy would say.

PEARL: Young guys don't go that way.

LETI: GHB.

PEARL: What?

LETI: Gammahydroxybutrate. Date rape, right into your Coca Cola. It breaks down real quick, very hard for labs to detect.

PEARL: You doped him?

LETI: He wanted to get married in the worst way and proposed at a Tony Roma's. I nearly collapsed from embarrassment. A fucking Tony Roma's! Worse, he wanted me to wear his mother's gown—designed for a hundred seven-five pound walking eggplant. I found the drugs in his bottom drawer and I wanted to turn the tables.

PEARL: Then you shoved him into the trunk.

LETI: 'Cause I couldn't fit him into the trash can. And I cut my hand along the trunk hinge. I borrowed the body bag from the E R in Mira Mesa. *(Pause)* Ralph had a coronary 'cause the G H B had cut off his respiration. It was his third heart attack. You could see how overweight this hippo was. Never thin enough for my eyes. But that's not the salient thing. He'd prowl around wherever I was. I couldn't get a crappy court order because he was tied to a big pro-life group. That's right. The judge was in their fucking pocket. Shit stacked so high—you wouldn't believe it. I just had to act. Pearl, having sex with him was like a grand slam match with the W W W F.

PEARL: You're scamming me.

LETI: Pumpkin?

PEARL: Your eyes twitch when it's a lie.

LETI: They twitch when I reach orgasm.

PEARL: I'm going to the cops.

LETI: Go ahead.

PEARL: *(Uncomfortable pause)* You're setting something up.

LETI: I've no reason to scam you. Can I be any more obvious?

PEARL: What? Forgetting him in the trunk?

LETI: Sure. I was going to drive far into the mountains and drop off his sorry ass. It was on my "must do list" along with a quick stop at Goodwill's garment box. I would have given most of the cash to Planned Parenthood. But it occurred to me that I was getting too complicated. And I don't trust myself when that happens. I get bad dreams. *(Pause)* You know, The Lady Or The Tiger... *(Pause)* It's a story about a test. Two doors. Pick one.

PEARL: Don't know it.

LETI: The guy has to choose. One door is a beautiful woman. The other door is death. The tiger.
See, if I left just the cash you would have run. But just the body, you go to the cops. Get it?
So I gave you both things. Something good, something bad. You had a choice.

PEARL: Oh...right...

LETI: *(Smiles)* So here we are. Why are you looking at me like that? Think the money's tainted? Maybe Ralphie's the dumb bagman for some asshole?

PEARL: *(Aware of the surroundings)* You're broadcasting to the entire block.

LETI: I don't care. These evil folks are right off the Interstate. They're going door to door and even have the P T A on a string. I swear, they threw out

Darwin and brought in a million dusty bibles. They've targeted abortion doctors from Minnesota to New Mexico. They're a gang of killers, darlin'. I didn't know everything about Ralph. Just a heating mechanic with a hernia. Simply blue collar. But he played me for a fool. Ralph was in the far right, wacko militia. They stop at nothing. And justify anything with a bullet.

PEARL: So you decided to take him out?

LETI: I wished him dead, yeah. We all do that sort of thing. But this was an innocent action.

PEARL: Take the car back, Leti

LETI: Ralph's gone. It was never his car.

PEARL: I don't want it.

LETI: You're untouched by him. He won't mess with you.

PEARL: Leti...

LETI: No ghosts going to bother you. Even if you spend that money. Just treat it like a gift.

PEARL: It's not a gift.

LETI: It's my gift to you. You know I like you.

PEARL: That doesn't help me. I should be completely hysterical.

LETI: Hysteria went out with the Beatles. I'm really sorry. Honest. *(Pause)* Why the hell did you come back?

PEARL: To return the car.

LETI: But you wanted to know what's inside me. Could you even be like me...

PEARL: I just wanted to return the fucking car.

LETI: O K. O K. Just leave it and get out of my face.

PEARL: I pity you, Leti.

LETI: Don't need your pity, girl.

PEARL: You need help.

LETI: Maybe I do.

PEARL: I'm not suggesting the police.

LETI: What? A psychiatric hospital by a nine hole golf course?

PEARL: Why not?

LETI: Ever see those low budget Roger Corman "women behind bars" films?

PEARL: No, but maybe I'll rent one.

LETI: There's always a chick like me—the classic misfit—trouble's double.

PEARL: I see now.

LETI: Maybe I'm a cult legend from the 1950s after all? *(Pause)* I can fix a delicious G H B cocktail for your boyfriend. A real gift. Wouldn't that be poetic?

PEARL: Fuck you.

LETI: It's true. What you want too. *(Pause)* I can read your mind.

PEARL: Get off my case.

LETI: Why don't you read mine? A two way looking glass. Close your eyes and try. *(Pause)* Come on. Try for little lamb-ikins.

PEARL: You want to kill Freddy.

LETI: He only abuses you.

PEARL: Freddy's not evil.

LETI: He is. Believe me. Just line up half the men on the planet.

PEARL: If you met him, you'd feel...

LETI: I doubt it. *(Pause)* Just for a moment—imagine that he's out of your life.

PEARL: No.

LETI: Try.

PEARL: You're creeping me out.

LETI: You'd be free and happier.

PEARL: So? Then it's up to me to walk away from him.

LETI: He won't let you.

PEARL: It's my choice.

LETI: Admit you need help.

PEARL: I know right from wrong.

LETI: There's only one real way to fight psychic domination, Pearl. You have to be a psychic. I'll teach you.

PEARL: I'd hate myself forever.

LETI: You'd get over it after a couple of hours.

PEARL: I've tried to quit him.

LETI: He stalks you.

PEARL: Yeah.

LETI: He comes inside drunk and bolts the door.

PEARL: Yeah.

LETI: If you told him it's absolutely over, he'd throw a monster tantrum.

PEARL: Men are men, Leti.

LETI: You'll get free. My prediction. *(Pause)* Ten years ago, I was just like you. Smoked a lot of pot, drank a ton of margaritas. Hitched across the country with eighty dollars in coins. Slept with a hundred underage guys. Wanted to see if they could be unique to me. Few were. Boys. Don't know why boys are in such a hurry, Pearl. There's no hurry. We're only going to be undone. We're school kids gone bad. Faster than the speed of light, growing older. Like me. Or like your mother. One or the other. Hope it's somebody you really want to be. 'Cause you only get to choose once.

PEARL: I did dream about you.

LETI: When?

PEARL: Last night. A vivid dream.

LETI: That's why you came back, Pearl.

PEARL: In my dream you looked younger. Revenge was inside your mouth. You took me to a chic boutique.

LETI: Yes, I can see it now.

PEARL: You watched me try on formal wear. The staff served champagne. We were drinking glass after glass and got giddy. I ripped my gown.

LETI: Such a minor tear.

PEARL: You bought the gown for me. It cost a fortune.

LETI: Arrange for me to meet Freddy.

PEARL: I can't.

LETI: It's so easy, Pearl.

PEARL: For you it is.

LETI: Royalty does this all the time. Look at British history. Look at French history.

PEARL: You believe in a supreme being?

LETI: I do.

PEARL: The angels will punish you.

LETI: Maybe not. There are a billion sinners crawling on this planet.

PEARL: More or less.

LETI: God is a woman. In the universe, she pees sitting down and tips the attendant generously. (Pause) But did God arrange for Freddy to tyrannize you?

PEARL: Who the hell knows?

LETI: Does God comfort you when you cry yourself to sleep?

PEARL: I wish. *(Pause)* The one time I left Freddy all hell broke loose.

LETI: Accept a favor. That's all it is, Pearl. *(Pause)* Please, Pearl.

PEARL: And in return?

LETI: In return...

PEARL: Yes...

LETI: You'll come with me to Rosarito Beach for a night or two. I love it there off season.

PEARL: I need to think it over.

LETI: Come on. I see your answer all over your sweet face.

PEARL: I get spooked in Mexico. All those aggressive Che Guevaras.

LETI: Che wasn't Mexico, honey. This is just over the border.

PEARL: For a weekend?

LETI: Sure.

PEARL: Drive down?

LETI: In our darlin' Mustang.

PEARL: When?

LETI: Right after I meet Mr. Freddy.

PEARL: I'll have to think about it— seriously.

LETI: Seriously? *(Pause)* Honestly, Pearl. I'll just meet him and get a bead on the situation.

PEARL: I need to cry myself to sleep.

LETI: *(Soothing)* All right.

PEARL: I feel like crying right now.

LETI: Then cry, sweet angel. I know the pain you've been in.

(Slowly PEARL hides her eyes with her hands.)

LETI: You don't have to be under his thumb. That's the goal, O K? Freedom. *(Pause)* Where does he work?

PEARL: At the Sears repair shop in Van Nuys. Every day but Monday.

LETI: Of course. O K. I'll take it from there.

PEARL: *(Beginning to cry)* If Freddy gets hurt, I'll probably go to Hell.

LETI: And I'll go with you to keep you company. Give me the keys to the Mustang. I'll take care of Ralph's body once and for all. I'll drop you off at the IHOP and get yourself some lunch. Back in an hour. O K? *(Pause)* There is no Hell, Pearl.

PEARL: How do you know?

LETI: There's only a hot Mohave desert right off the freeway. Real Hell is getting screwed by your stepfather against the kitchen sink. . *(Pause)* I won't do anything cruel.

PEARL: O K.

LETI: OK.

(Tender smile between them)

LETI: And don't forget to pack a swim suit with your long string of matching cultured pearls. We'll have a silly, cozy night-over in Rosarito.

(End of scene)

Scene Four

(LETI *drives* PEARL *along the coastal toll road in Mexico.*
PEARL *holds a valentine's box of chocolate candies.*)

LETI: O K, so Barry Bonds hit his 73rd homer. Breaks
Maguire's record, who broke Maris' record, who broke
Babe Ruth's record. O K. The ball's easily worth a
million bucks.

PEARL: O K.

LETI: Are you with me?

PEARL: Yeah.

LETI: This Russian guy Alex Popov catches the ball
with a mitt. The crowd in the bleachers rush him.
  He loses the fucking ball. O K?

PEARL: O K.

LETI: This Japanese guy Patrick Hayashi grabs it, tucks
the ball inside his pocket. The Russian claims this guy
bit him. What do you think happens?

PEARL: I don't know. The Japanese guy goes out to
party?

LETI: No.

PEARL: The crowd beats up both guys.

LETI: No.

PEARL: The Russian guy hires a hit man?

LETI: They go to court. The judge rules in favor of both
men. O K?

PEARL: O K.

LETI: You'd think an American fan would catch the
goddamn ball. O K. So joint custody over a baseball.
Either these two assholes have to cash in and split the
sale, or pay the other asshole a half million for the ball.
Just like biblical Solomon and the baby cut in two.

LETI & PEARL: *(Sing in unison)*
Pony car, pony car
Won't you be my pony car?
Don't say no
Here we go
Ride across the plain
Carry me, marry me
Come away with me!
Giddy up, giddy up!
Come away with me.

PEARL: This is so gross.

LETI: What?

PEARL: You left two pieces. All the rest are half chewed.

LETI: I hardly touched them.

PEARL: Come on.

LETI: I don't like fruit filling. I only like caramel or nuts.

PEARL: That's disgusting.

LETI: No, no, no...the fruity stuff was made for another kind of person.

PEARL: This was a new box an hour ago.

LETI: O K. O K.

PEARL: Where did you bury Freddy?

LETI: At the outskirts of a San Ysidro dude ranch. One hour rides under twenty-five bucks.

PEARL: You're not so cool, Leti.

LETI: So?

PEARL: Little kids go there.

LETI: Good weed?

PEARL: What?

LETI: Good weed? I like it when the seeds pop.

PEARL: So do I.

LETI: Kinda silly.

PEARL: Kinda kooky.

LETI: Kinda dopey.

PEARL: Kinda loopy.

LETI: That was the last joint?

PEARL: Yep.

LETI: Oh no!

PEARL: That's why I want a real piece of chocolate.

LETI: I'll buy you a Hershey bar. O K?

PEARL: It's not the same.

LETI: You know these Mexican cops will fuck us brutally just to find a dinky roach clip. Ten years in a lice diseased jail without premium cable.

PEARL: I'm clean, doll-face.

LETI: What did you call me?

PEARL: Doll-face.

LETI: That's not O K.

PEARL: My mother called me that all the time.

LETI: Doll-face?

PEARL: Never mind.

LETI: I'm not your fucking mother.

PEARL: I didn't say you were.

LETI: I'm sure your mother's ten years older than me.

PEARL: Yeah.

LETI: At least.

PEARL: Definitely. Why don't you let me drive?

LETI: You'll drive on the way back.

PEARL: Oh, come on, Leti. It's my car.

LETI: I'll put the radio on.

PEARL: Don't.

LETI: What's wrong now?

PEARL: I'm gonna cry.

LETI: Don't cry. You can't cry. You're fucking stoned.

PEARL: I gotta cry.

LETI: 'Cause what I said?

PEARL: What did you say?

LETI: Doll-face.

PEARL: That's what my mother used to say. My mom would sew my name into all my labels. Crazy. I never lost a blouse. I never lost a button. But she knew how to shake me down, you know. She knew what to say. She knew the game. She knew when I got scared. So she called me doll-face. And all I could do was stare like a Barbie doll. *(Pause)* Do you like the Go Gos or the Bangles?

LETI: Is there a difference?

PEARL: Do you like Diet Pepsi or Coke?

LETI: What do you think?

PEARL: Do you like short kisses or long hugs?

LETI: Sugar is sugar.

PEARL: And spice is spice.

LETI: Sugar is not spice.

PEARL: Weatherman said there'd be a meteor shower tonight.

LETI: Worth staying up for?

PEARL: Yeaaaaaaaaaaaaah...

LETI: OK.

PEARL: OK.

LETI: If I catch a falling star, I'll give it to you.

PEARL: Why?

LETI: *(Serene smile)* Because I'm falling too.

(End of scene)

Scene Five

(Seedy Rosarito Beach hotel balcony. Evening. PEARL is sipping a margarita while talking to LETI—still inside room)

PEARL: There's a wonderful shower tonight.

LETI: *(Off stage)* Really?

PEARL: You got to see this.

LETI: *(Off stage)* I've one more phone call to make.

PEARL: Hurry. The call can wait.

LETI: *(Off stage)* I've seen meteorites before.

PEARL: This one's spectacular!

(LETI joins PEARL.)

PEARL: Look to your right. Oooooohhh....

LETI: *(Impressed)* We'll order room service. This is a show.

PEARL: *(Noticing LETI's flamboyant dress)* Where did that come from?

LETI: Packed under the wind breaker.

PEARL: *(Attention back on the sky)* A little conspicuous for this resort.

LETI: I wouldn't call this a resort, cupcake. You met the clientele in the lobby.

PEARL: Some senior group off a vagrant bus.

LETI: You gave them a false name. Enya Celine?

PEARL: We're paying with cash.

LETI: I realize.

PEARL: My way of keeping private.

LETI: Are you going to wear that to dinner?

PEARL: It's a Calvin Klein knock-off.

LETI: At least you can fix up your hair.

PEARL: It's the gorgeous humidity.

LETI: You've lovely rich hair, Pearl.

PEARL: What did you buy downstairs?

LETI: A bottle of wine. There are three Consuelas—two working the gift shop and one managing the beauty salon. It's like hitting the jackpot at a slot machine!

PEARL: Merlot?

LETI: Pinot Noir.

(PEARL *smiles.*)

LETI: Want some?

PEARL: I feel lighter than a feather.

LETI: Good or bad?

PEARL: A good feather.

LETI: A good feather friend.

PEARL: Did you ever hold a job, Leti?

LETI: Ahuh.

PEARL: What sort of job?

LETI: *(Pouring wine)* I was a dental assistant.

PEARL: Oh, come on...

LETI: "You don't have to floss all your teeth, just the ones you want to keep."

PEARL: When?

LETI: A year ago.

PEARL: Where?

LETI: L A.

PEARL: How long?

LETI: Long enough to make me flip out.

PEARL: Did you quit?

LETI: I was prompt, pert, and perfect—all girlie skills a little hygienist needs.

I tucked in those people nice and neat, asked them to spit and rinse with a tiny disposable wine glass. The dentist had these dumb gimmicks. The most repetitive goddamn thing I ever did in my life.

PEARL: I worked nights in a law firm proofing documents. Twenty dollars an hour and they didn't take out taxes. I stayed up all night. You just force yourself to push on. The world came into focus at the firm. Every deal was a battle. That's the nature of written law.

LETI: You sound so smart.

PEARL: I'm dancing along.

LETI: Dancing keeps you young.

PEARL: Nice wine. *(Continues to sip)* I read a lot. I like to read.

LETI: If you're so smart, how did you take up with Freddy boy?

PEARL: Blame my horoscope. I do.

LETI: He pursued you from the get go.

PEARL: Yeah.

LETI: But you gave him permission.

PEARL: I gave him a chance. That's all a person can ask.

LETI: Everyone has two sides.

PEARL: He's invisible now.

LETI: Is he?

PEARL: I can still hear his voice. When he was on good behavior it was like magic.

LETI: Such love is magic.

PEARL: Laugh if you want. I believe in magic.

LETI: So do I.

PEARL: Oh, my head's spinning so.

LETI: The wine?

PEARL: No, the lights ahead.

LETI: Close your eyes.

(PEARL *does.* LETI *studies her face.*)

LETI: I'm glad that you trust me.

PEARL: I don't.

LETI: You will in time.

PEARL: Trust takes time. *(Pause)* Do you trust me?

LETI: I think so.

PEARL: I better stop drinking.

LETI: What's your worry?

PEARL: You might hurt me.

LETI: Not in a million years.

PEARL: Sometimes my mother would do hurtful things to me.

LETI: I understand.

PEARL: Do you really?

LETI: As best I can.

PEARL: And I'm trying to forgive her.

LETI: That would be generous of you.

PEARL: *(Opening her eyes)* Did you put anything in my glass?

LETI: Nothing.

PEARL: Swear to me.

LETI: I swear, Pearl.

PEARL: Last thing I want is to wake up dead cold wearing a cheap tattoo.

LETI: *(Laughing gently)* You crack me up.

PEARL: What did you tell Ralph's mother—before leaving?

LETI: Said I wasn't coming back.

PEARL: You packed up everything?

LETI: Everything I could take in two arms.

PEARL: Must have been harder than that.

LETI: Maybe it was. Do you really care?

PEARL: I do. Are we're at risk?

LETI: For what?

PEARL: For a streak of supernaturally bad luck.

LETI: No.

PEARL: I think we are.

LETI: That's so fucking morbid.

PEARL: What about an incurable disease that you read about in National Geographic?

LETI: Absurd.

PEARL: A disease doesn't have to inhabit your blood stream.

LETI: There's a kick of a headline.

PEARL: When you breath the steamy hot air of another

LETI: Yes...

PEARL: When you take in every whispered word

LETI: Yes...

PEARL: When you accidently brush a hand against a naked arm...

LETI: I know. Or the smallest finger...

PEARL: *(Pause)*

What the hell am I doing here?

LETI: You want good things to come true.

PEARL: Here?

LETI: Yes, here in Baja.

PEARL: Baja sounds like a little injured lamb in a children's book.

LETI: So why not write that beautiful little book? Or... why not just order lobster? I know you're famished.

PEARL: Leti, I fear I have a nasty mental disease.

LETI: If you do, then you really must try the lobster.

PEARL: Please take me seriously.

LETI: I do.

PEARL: Don't you think the cops will come?

LETI: No.

PEARL: Eventually they will.

LETI: I doubt it.

PEARL: I expect them. *(Attention back on the night sky)* The sky's gone black. Not a meteor in sight. And I feel so insignificant and small.

LETI: Another glass? *(About to pour)*

PEARL: No.

LETI: Are you tired?

PEARL: Ahuh.

LETI: Do you want to lie down and rest?

PEARL: Maybe for a few minutes. Thank you.

LETI: Do you want me to leave you here?

PEARL: What, you take the car?

LETI: That's not what I meant.

PEARL: What did you mean?

LETI: I don't want the car.

PEARL: You don't want to leave me.

LETI: I don't.

PEARL: You're just saying that to be perverse.

LETI: That's such a strong word, darling.

PEARL: Is it?

LETI: Sometimes I am perverse. Not now, angel.

PEARL: Neither am I.

LETI: So get some rest. I'll be right back.

PEARL:

Deep down I'm just like country fair apple pie.

LETI: I like apple pie.

PEARL: So do I. With a topping of ice cream.

(As LETI's about to exit)

PEARL: How did you get Fred to meet you at the IHOP?

LETI: It wasn't hard.

PEARL: But tell me.

LETI: I called his shop a couple of times...

PEARL: And?

LETI:...and I mentioned your name. Geez, it's like telemarketing.

PEARL: He's so gullible.

LETI: Ahuh.

PEARL: You met him that day?

LETI: No. The next day.

PEARL: But he didn't call me.

LETI: Why should he?

PEARL: Check things with me?

LETI: I said we should keep it a secret. *(Pause)* We were arranging a surprise birthday for you.

PEARL: He didn't remember my birthday?

LETI: Guess not.

PEARL: Everyone forgets my birthday. *(Pause)* What happened at the IHOP?

LETI: Screaming fucking bratty kids—makes Chucky Cheese look like The Fucking Four Seasons.

PEARL: What did you order?

LETI: Pearl?

PEARL: Come on.

LETI: I had the Belgian waffles. He had a stack of silver dollar pancakes. He polished off my waffles.

PEARL: What did you talk about?

LETI: This and that. Tanya Harding's spectacular new boxing career and Mickey Rourke's botched plastic surgery. He seemed really interested in me. My blouse was nearly open down to my belt. It was Saturday and I had make-up on. His leg stroked against mine. Need more details?

PEARL: Yeah.

LETI: He asked about any boyfriends. I said I wasn't seeing anyone since The Eurythmics disbanded. That made him laugh. He never heard of them. He said that you never mentioned me.

PEARL: Did he fidget with his motorcycle ring?

LETI: He did.

PEARL: You weren't bored?

LETI: I like anthropology. *(Leaning over the balcony rail)* Sure, he looked stupid, vain and boyish. I should have left him right there. My fucking ambivalence. I didn't know what to do. He asked a few things about you. Intimate things. He insisted on seeing me that night. He wrote down my phone number and would drive down from L A. He promised me a marathon orgasm. But I could see his expiration date along his blockhead. And for a moment, I thought he could see me laughing inside. He followed me to his death in La Jolla.

PEARL: You didn't care?

LETI: I did care. He wouldn't have been on the prowl otherwise.

PEARL: You let him kiss you?

LETI: Yeah.

PEARL: More than once?

LETI: A couple of times. But my lips were tight.

PEARL: Why?

LETI: To gain his trust.

PEARL: And then?

LETI: Didn't I tell you this before? *(Pause)* Ralph's mother was gone for the weekend. I was totally alone. *(Pause)* Your boy had a lot on his mind. Crap about his band, his money worries, you...

PEARL: So you just sat there...

LETI: Drinking a beer or two.

PEARL: What he say about me?

LETI: Does it matter?

PEARL: Yeah.

LETI: That you bossed him around too much...in bed.

PEARL: He didn't say that shit.

LETI: It was his way of getting sympathy.

PEARL: What a turd.

LETI: He got something in the bargain.

PEARL: Like what?

LETI: A merciful embrace and then...

PEARL: You spiked his beer.

LETI: He felt nothing.

PEARL: Nothing?

LETI: Nothing.

PEARL: And then?

LETI: I turned on the TV and found an old movie while Freddy slept. Starring Cary Grant in *An Affair To Reguritate*...

PEARL: Unbelievable...

LETI: Later I put a mirror to Fred's mouth. Wide as Arizona and what cavities. The drug took effect. That moment I felt his soul left his body.

PEARL: You should be crying.

LETI: I draped his body along the sofa and covered him with a fitted sheet. I'm not making anything up. I swear to you. All true.

PEARL: How can you hurt someone you don't know?

LETI: I didn't hurt him, Pearl. He slipped away so
gently. *(Pause)* I was exhausted and had to sleep. So I
left and checked into the Holiday Inn. It would have
been impossible to spend the night with dear departed
Freddy. As it turned out, when I made it back into the
house, Mrs Kroeger—Ralph's mother—was coming
up the driveway. Earlier than expected. I rushed to the
door and kept her from coming into the living room.
The old gal was feeling ill and needed to lie in bed. I
gave her a bouquet for Mother's Day. Then I went to
fix her some lunch and afterwards, when she took a
nap, I packed a shovel and got rid of Freddy. He was
much lighter than my Ralphie and off he went into my
rented Toyota Camry.

PEARL: You really did it?

LETI: As God is my witness.

PEARL: Oh my gosh...

LETI: I'm sorry, Pearl.

PEARL: This is totally insane.

LETI: It's going to be O K, honey.

PEARL: How?

LETI: As the French say, *"fait accompli"* —the deed is
done.

PEARL: But are you're sure he's dead?

LETI: A hundred percent sure. I buried him.

PEARL: Take me there.

LETI: Oh, that would be dumb.

PEARL: I have to go.

LETI: Why?

PEARL: Just take me there. Maybe he's only numb.

LETI: He's deader than Elvis. *(Pause)* I assume all of your guilt. And don't worry, his grunge band will find a new drummer.

PEARL: Dear angels overhead, forgive us for our crimes.

LETI: Want to go to church?

PEARL: No.

LETI: I'll go with you.

PEARL: Am I dreaming?

LETI: No.

PEARL: Fred always liked coming to Baja.

LETI: Really?

PEARL: His other passion was fishing.

LETI: Maybe a sea burial would have been the thing?

PEARL: I can't even think anymore.

LETI: I don't want you to hurt, Pearl. So just let it all go. This man was your demon. Now he's gone. *(Pause)* Let's go down for dinner.

PEARL: I can't eat.

LETI: Sure you can.

(LETI *tries to put an arm over* PEARL, *but is shunned.*)

PEARL: I need to be alone.

LETI: Don't despise me, Pearl.

PEARL: I don't know what to think anymore.

LETI: We can become best friends.

PEARL: I don't see how.

LETI: I'm not a dangerous person to my friends.

PEARL: You have no friends.

LETI: I'm selective, that's true.

PEARL: You have no lovers.

LETI: That's so cruel of you.

PEARL: I don't know what to think anymore. *(Pause)* It's getting cold.

LETI: Take my shawl. *(Removes it from her shoulders)*

PEARL: Where did you get that?

LETI: At the shop downstairs. Very Spanish?

PEARL: *(Puts it on)* Yeah.

LETI: I could buy you beautiful clothes. It would be a kick So much fun. Shop all day in Ensenada. My Mom loved to dress me when I was a teen. The only way we got along. Somehow she was blessed with good taste.

PEARL: In clothes?

LETI: Cancer. She passed away five years ago. And your mother?

PEARL: My Mom's in Long Beach.

LETI: Too close?

PEARL: I suppose.

LETI: *(Gently sarcastic)* Want to phone her?

PEARL: Why?

LETI: Wish her a Happy Mother's Day?

(PEARL shakes her head.)

PEARL: She's living with a retired professional bowler.

LETI: That's so cool.

(The hotel room phone rings.)

PEARL: Don't answer it.

LETI: Why not?

PEARL: Who'd be calling?

LETI: Room service? Maybe it's your Mom? *(Picks up phone)* Yes? *(Pause)* What? *(Pause)* I can't understand you. *No comprendo todo, verdad. (To* PEARL*)* Did you call for a doctor?

PEARL: No.

LETI: *(To phone caller)* You have the wrong room. *El numero incorrecto! (Hangs up)*

PEARL: Do you understand Spanish?

LETI: *(Flip)* Not really.

PEARL: I don't feel safe here.

LETI: I understand, sweetie. You can size up a joint by its room service. *(Realizing the wine is gone)* Think we need to get a couple of margaritas downstairs. There's a lounge show right after dinner. That'll take your mind away. Let's go.

PEARL: I'm not going to sleep with you.

LETI: What?

PEARL: You heard me.

LETI: Why are you saying that?

PEARL: I don't know.

LETI: What the hell's wrong with you?

PEARL: In case you've expectations.

LETI: I have no expectations.

PEARL: You do.

LETI: You're way off base, Pearl.

PEARL: The room has only one bed.

LETI: So? *(Pause)* You were there when we checked in. That was all they had.

PEARL: You could have asked for a cot or a roller bed.

LETI: I'll sleep on the goddamn couch.

PEARL: It's not big enough.

LETI: Honey, get off my case, O K? I've slept in hammocks, on park benches, and three legged bar stools. If I'm creeping you out, then we better separate here and now.

PEARL: You're not creeping me out.

LETI: Then act like you believe that.

PEARL: The desk clerk gave me a glance. Like he knew.

LETI: Like he knew what?

PEARL: That we were different from the others.

LETI: That's because we used a coupon at check in.

PEARL: But he gave you the room key and whistled.

LETI: Well, fuck him. This is not The Hoi Poloi at Palm Springs. The help makes five bucks on a good day.

PEARL: I can't.

LETI: Everything between us is very innocent. That's all I know. That's all people need to know. That's what I'm comfortable with. Yes, I do like you. From the moment we met. I think it's mutual, Pearl. And in the process of getting to know each other, we did each other a sublime favor. The men in our lives have gone and soon I'll get to Cabo. Maybe with you, maybe not. *(Pause)* You didn't have to come. You're full of mixed messages. You must know. And you can drive a person insane. I trust you, Pearl. I don't trust people. I wouldn't have sold my car to you, otherwise. I wouldn't be sharing a hotel room with you. And I sure wouldn't have committed a criminal action without your support.

(Aware of PEARL's lingering discomfort)

LETI: I don't sleep with women. I don't seduce people. I don't do things out of the norm. I'm just an average American girl looking for joy.

PEARL: I understand.

LETI: I hope you do.

PEARL: I'm sorry.

LETI: I am too.

PEARL: Maybe I drank too much.

LETI: Maybe.

PEARL: Maybe I'm paranoid.

LETI: Smart people usually are.

PEARL: What about the money you left in the Mustang?

LETI: It's yours to spend.

PEARL: No strings?

LETI: I don't see any strings.

PEARL: I want to believe you, Leti.

LETI: So believe me. As they say in Tijuana—"Ya basta!" What's rattling inside your head?

PEARL: It suddenly hit me—I'm free of Freddy.

LETI: And if there's a Heaven, he'll play drums all the time. *(Walking towards the front door)* When I was six years old, I could see my wedding day. So perfect. My gown would be ice cream vanilla with red roses everywhere. I could see the gorgeous groom too. He looked a little like you, Pearl. Man's body. I guess that makes no sense at all. The face is everything. You can see the soul. *(Pause)* Know why people whisper?

PEARL: Why?

LETI: So they can be seriously heard. *(Opens the door)* I know you'll be leaving tomorrow after breakfast. I read you like a book. It's your choice. The evening could be unforgettable. I could go forever on a good feeling. Maybe I don't deserve anything lasting. I reserved an outside table. Tonight you judge.

PEARL: I can't judge you.

LETI: You can't help but judge.

(LETI *exits.* PEARL *remains.*)

(*End of scene*)

Scene Five

(*Exterior dining at the hotel.* LETI *and* PEARL *are seated, drinking margaritas.* LETI *holds an unlit cigarette.*)

PEARL: While you were in the restroom, a man came over to our table.

LETI: What did he want?

PEARL: He asked me about my necklace. He noticed us at check-in. He admired our Mustang.

LETI: American?

PEARL: Mexican.

LETI: What did you say?

PEARL: I said I liked wearing pearls. Or something stupid like that.

LETI: Why say anything? (*Picking up her menu*)

PEARL: What should I have said? I like pearls.

LETI: Did you order?

PEARL: Lobster.

LETI: For both of us?

PEARL: Ahuh.

(LETI *starts to light cigarette.*)

PEARL: Don't smoke.

LETI: Helps me to relax.

PEARL: It wasn't a big deal, Leti.

LETI: I know.

PEARL: We don't have to eat here.

LETI: Forget it.

PEARL: We can go elsewhere.

LETI: Where is he?

PEARL: That guy who came by... *(Pause)* Sitting inside by himself. Right by the piano. Wearing a large grey cowboy hat and a white carnation.

(LETI turns to look.)

PEARL: He told me he's a cop.

LETI: *(Skeptical)* That's such bullshit.

PEARL: Why would he lie?

LETI: So gullible, Pearl. Cops don't wear flowers.

PEARL: He showed me his badge.

LETI: They buy tin badges in Tijuana's barrios. That jerk looks like a peasant farmer from Guadalajara.

PEARL: He says his brother Luis is one of the owners of the hotel.

LETI: And I'm Donald Trump's love child.

PEARL: He gave me his card. *(Showing LETI)* See. It says *"policia secreto"*.

LETI: Ahuh.

PEARL: That means he's a detective.

LETI: *(Flip)* And he tells lots of *"secretos"* to young little American girls?

PEARL: Yeah. Maybe he does.

LETI: Great.

PEARL: He's married nineteen years. His wife has leukemia. They had a telethon for her last month and raised thirty thousand dollars.

LETI: I was gone for two minutes...

PEARL: He's very chatty. He loves *Sex And The City* on H B O's Spanish channel. He said I was prettier than Sarah Jessica Parker no matter what rags she wears.

LETI: Honey, half the women on this planet are prettier than that fucking spoiled ditz.

PEARL: You're afraid of Mexican cops?

LETI: I am.

PEARL: Do you think Mexican cops are pigs?

LETI: I've seen a few swine. *(Pause)*

Let's not be really stupid this side of the border.

PEARL: The dude's just another asshole in a ten gallon hat. He thought we were sisters. *(Pause)* I don't understand. You've so much cool back home.

LETI: Mexican cops are worse than Mexican thieves. If he is a cop. He probably knows our room number.

PEARL: I didn't tell him.

LETI: So his wife has polio...

PEARL: He showed me her photo. She looks very ill. They're trying acupuncture now. *(Pause)* He owns a '68 Mustang. He loves Mustangs. Says a lot of them are stolen from L A and taken

to Tijuana. The cars go to chop shops and sold for parts all over the U S. We can put a club on the steering wheel, the thieves will still strip the car bare. He swears that a Saint Christopher on the dash will protect us from a violent carjacking.

LETI: I detest Saint Christopher.

PEARL: I guess we could go with a rabbit's foot.

LETI: He just wants to pick you up.

PEARL: Do you think I look that gullible?

LETI: I didn't say that.

PEARL: But that's the...

LETI: He's looking right at you.

PEARL: Oh shit.

LETI: This is nothing but trouble.

PEARL: I'll walk up and tell him to go screw himself with a front axel.

(PEARL *half rises as* LETI *grabs* PEARL's *hand.*)

PEARL: What?

LETI: Don't be a pain in the ass. We both need a little rest.

PEARL: I know.

LETI: Turn your chair so he can't see you.

(PEARL *does.*)

LETI: O K.

PEARL: What if he checks our car tomorrow?

LETI: We'll clean it out tonight—for any illicit drugs.

PEARL: He reminds me of my grade school gym teacher with that hounddog face.

LETI: And that sparked the connection?

PEARL: You're becoming my mother.

LETI: Is this what happens to you after a few drinks? Tell me—when you go back to L A, how will you handle questions about your ex?

PEARL: I don't know.

LETI: Think for a second.

PEARL: You mean when friends ask? (*Pause*) I suppose I'll avoid answering any questions.

LETI: And if the cops investigate?

PEARL: I haven't a lot to tell them.

LETI: Would you mention my name? Your car purchase, trips to San Diego, Fred's disappearance...

PEARL: I've only a few things of his. Some C Ds and a fabulous mauve shirt from the Gap.

LETI: He might have talked to someone before his drive.

PEARL: I doubt it.

LETI: But you can't be sure. So think the worst. I do. *(Pause)* I thought you'd be more attentive.

PEARL: I know how to be attentive. *(Pause)* You snuffed my ex-boyfriend, Leti. I could have stopped you. I should have.

LETI: Are you depressed now?

PEARL: I think so.

LETI: You don't look depressed.

PEARL: I'm in pain.

LETI: You miss him.

PEARL: I don't know.

(PEARL notices something in LETI's face.)

PEARL: What?

LETI: He's coming over.

PEARL: The cop?

LETI: Whoever the fuck he is.

PEARL: Don't scare the little guy. It's his country.

LETI: *(Whispers)* Shut up.

PEARL: *(Whistpers)* Leti...

LETI: *(Directly at him, although we can't see him)* Yes? *(Pause)* Can I help you? *(Pause)* I said...can I help you?

Puedo ayudarle? Digame, tonto—por favor? (Pause) Then
beat it. *Vaya, tu pinga!* Quit staring, schmuck.

(LETI and PEARL both watch him leave.)

PEARL: *(Whisters)* Why did you have to piss him off?

LETI: I'm not a piece of meat.

PEARL: Did he say you were?

LETI: He didn't have to when men scratch their crotch
and look you in the eye.

Let's go upstairs. I'm exhausted.

PEARL: But...

LETI: We'll have the food sent to our room.

PEARL: He's about to leave the restaurant, Leti. I can
feel it.

LETI: You can feel a cop, or you can cop a feel. Your
choice.

(Mariachi music is heard.)

LETI: It's in the cologne, Pearl. When all else fails, smell
the cheap cologne.

PEARL: We've done nothing wrong in Baja.

LETI: In Baja.

PEARL: The Mustang's street legal. *(Pause)* I'm going
back to L A in the morning. I need to return to things I
know.

LETI: We can't leave just yet.

PEARL: Why not?

LETI: I scheduled a facial and a peel.

PEARL: *(Dryly sarcastic)* Oh?

LETI: We can't leave this moment. He'll a smell a rat.

PEARL: I don't care.

LETI: You don't get it, do you? A daughter of a cop.

PEARL: I'm uncomfortable.

LETI: And so am I, doll face. *(Pause)* There are cops that punch the clock for a clean pisspot and for candy ass stripes... *(Picks up her margarita glass in the air)* And very filthy cops who get filthy rich the filthy way and play God Almighty with your life *(Sips margarita)* So this fake Jose-Pedro-Manuel-Alfonso-Fuck-Face has a hunch about us. We check out tomorrow, Monday, before lunch.

PEARL: O K.

LETI: O K?

PEARL: And if he sneaks up on me?

(LETI stares quietly at PEARL.)

PEARL: Do I play dumb? What if he drags me to headquarters?

LETI: He only wants to screw you, Pearl. And you probably encouraged him. *(Finishing her drink)* I'll tell the waiter to bring the fucking lobster to our room. *(Rises to exit)*

PEARL: And I'm supposed to jump up and follow you?

LETI: *(Delicate and rather sincere)* No. Jumping is not ladylike. Not in La Jolla, and definitely not in Mexico.

(End of scene)

Scene Six

(Later that night in the hotel room. PEARL begins to undress while LETI sits in a chair by the open balcony.)

PEARL: There's a search light on the ocean. A beautiful effect...like a magician's wand sweeping thieves clean.

LETI: It's the Mexican Coast Guard.

PEARL: Oh. *(Pause)* On Prom Night, my date and I danced half the night at a place just like this. He was stuck on a Swedish girl new to our school. She talked to the boys in perfect English. It was like she was doing every guy but my guy. And that made him very uptight. We got into an argument about her on Prom Night and I had to walk home after two A M. In heels. Five endless miles.

LETI: You look different suddenly.

PEARL: It taught me a lesson and he got to undo my lace bra.

LETI: Lucky boy.

PEARL: *(Having removed her jewelry, she unbuttons her blouse)* Did you go to your Prom?

LETI: No. Aren't you cold?

PEARL: With the balcony open I am.

LETI: Put your clothes back on.

PEARL: Are you sure?

LETI: You don't want to catch a chill.

PEARL: Maybe there'll be more shooting stars. I forgot to make a wish. *(Reads a folded newspaper)* Christie's auction house in New York is selling all of Marilyn Monroe's personals—her blue jeans from *River Of No Return* thirty-seven thousand dollars, her "Happy Birthday, Mister President" dress, her DiMaggio 34 diamond wedding ring seven hundred thousand dollars, her annotated Christian Bible thirty-three thousand dollars, her Union Jewish Prayerbook forty thousand dollars. *(Pause)* That's kind of weird, a Jewish book fetched seven thousand dollars more than the New Testament. *(Reading to herself)* She converted when she met Arthur Miller. Poor baby. He probably forced her.

LETI: What are you going to do with the money?

PEARL: I...I don't know.

LETI: You've had time to think about it.

PEARL: Yeah. *(Pause)* You said it was mine to keep.

LETI: That's right.

PEARL: All of it. Why are you looking at me that way?

LETI: Your face has changed.

PEARL: I could get my eyes redone. I heard of a good plastic surgeon in Bel Air who accepts cash.

LETI: You're too young for plastic surgery.

PEARL: I never liked my eyes.

LETI: I like your eyes

PEARL: Great.

LETI: *(After an awkward silence)* Time to go to sleep. I'm exhausted.

PEARL: You look it.

LETI: Don't change, Pearl. I mean it. You're nearly perfect.

PEARL: I'm wide awake. I got to walk around.

LETI: No.

PEARL: Leti...

LETI: Stay in the room, even if you can't sleep. In case the creep...

PEARL: Is strolling about...

LETI: You'll be on your own, darling. Don't break my heart.

PEARL: O K.

LETI: O K?

PEARL: O K. *(Back reading the paper)* "Death by Wired Bras"...London. The death of two women last month by a bolt of lighting in Hyde Park was due to their underwire bras serving as conductors, a coroner said today. "I think this was a tragic case, a pure act of Heaven," the coroner said at an inquest. The women, Anuban Bell, twenty-four, and Sunee Whitworth, thirty-nine, had found shelter under a tree during a severe thunderstorm. *(Pause)* Imagine that? In a thunder storm, why would any smart girl wear metal around her tits?

(End of scene)

Scene Seven

(The next morning in the hotel room. PEARL is waking from under the bed blanket. she looks around, not seeing LETI.)

PEARL: Leti? *(Pause)* Leti?

LETI: *(Off stage)* I'm in the bathroom.

PEARL: Oh.

LETI: *(Off stage)* I just got up.

PEARL: What time is it?

LETI: Just after nine.

PEARL: I'm flat out dead.

LETI: *(Entering)* I can tell you didn't sleep. *(Throws her jacket on the couch)* I was on the wicker couch.

PEARL: The couch?

LETI: That thing.

PEARL: Ouch!

LETI: I got to sleep.

PEARL: I had the weirdest dreams in a long time.

LETI: Good weird or bad?

PEARL: I don't know. I woke up soaked in sweat. I was a kid of eight. Away at summer camp. One of the chubby kids hung from the flag pole. Gruesome. They always hang the chubby ones.

LETI: Do you walk in your sleep, Pearl?

PEARL: Did I?

LETI: You left the room.

PEARL: You're kidding.

LETI: Yeah, you did.

PEARL: In my nightgown?

LETI: No, you got dressed. Shoes and all.

PEARL: Where did I go?

LETI: You don't remember?

PEARL: No. How did I get back in the room?

LETI: I guess you had the key with you.

PEARL: And I always lose room keys. *(Pause)* You watched me come and go?

LETI: Ahuh.

PEARL: It didn't freak you out?

LETI: No.

PEARL: Why didn't you stop me?

LETI: That 'wive's tale' that one mustn't ever wake up a sleepwalker—unless the dreamer is about to risk injury. It provokes the nocturnal ghost.

PEARL: What ghost?

LETI: The ghost which leads the dreamer.

PEARL: No one led me.

LETI: Did you dream of Fred?

PEARL: I did.

LETI: He came to you.

PEARL: Yeah, I think so...laughing his head off. How strange is that? I told him he was killed in a terrible accident. "What accident?" he said.

LETI: Did you phone him?

PEARL: What?

LETI: Did you phone him?

PEARL: *(Silence)* Did I?

LETI: Answer yes or no.

PEARL: I dialed his number. Yes.

LETI: I thought so.

PEARL: In my dream.

LETI: No, you phoned him from the hotel lobby.

PEARL: How do you know?

LETI: I followed you.

PEARL: *(Seeming more awake. Getting dressed)* I spoke to his brother. Freddy isn't dead.

LETI: His brother?

PEARL: He's got a brother dumber than a rock.

LETI: What did he say?

PEARL: The band's dumping him. *(Pause)* You fucked Fred.

LETI: Did his brother say that?

PEARL: Yeah. He's really pissed off.

LETI: Freddy or his brother?

PEARL: You're fucking unbelievable! I told him everything.

LETI: You told the dumb brother we're at this hotel?

PEARL: Yeah.

LETI: You're playing with me.

PEARL: No.

LETI: Why are you being so awful?

PEARL: You poisoned Fred, but the dose wasn't enough. Was that deliberate?

LETI: I tried to kill him. You know that.

PEARL: And you had the gall to fuck him first.

LETI: I don't like men any more. You know that.

PEARL: *(Not listening deliberately)* You just can't fuck people for sport.

LETI: I don't fuck people, Pearl!

PEARL: I loved him some days. And that's the truth, Leti.

LETI: Why lie to me, Pearl?

PEARL: *(Walking around to collect her things)* I'm telling the truth. Something which escapes you.

LETI: I don't fuck people and I don't lie. I imagine the truth. I call it poetry.

PEARL: Say no more, Leti. I'm going.

LETI: He made moves. Undressed me. I made the better move. I gave him medicine. You gave your consent. He passed out. The rest was up to Providence.

PEARL: So the asshole played dead for an hour.

LETI: This was different from Ralph.

PEARL: You're a sick puppy, Leti.

LETI: Twenty minutes later he was waking up. Scared the shit out of me. I nearly had a coronary. A guy his size should have stayed under with that dose. I ran.

PEARL: No. Nothing adds up with you.

LETI: I don't think you can quit the boy.

PEARL: I have a life free from him. Now.

LETI: So you're angry with me because I didn't kill him?

PEARL: Bullshit.

LETI: You want something from me, but you're afraid.

PEARL: Bullshit. I went out a second time. Just before dawn.

LETI: What?

PEARL: You were snoring louder than a firehouse and I couldn't sleep. Thinking about Freddy and your vicious lies. The lobby stank of cigars and I ended up in the parking lot. Staring at the Mustang. That cop came sneaking up behind me. He had your purse Leti. You must have forgotten it at the table. He popped it open and found a makeup box with grass inside. Yes, my make-up box. He smiled.

LETI: That's cute.

PEARL: I have good fate. You don't.

LETI: What's that supposed to mean?

PEARL: It was how you wrote that classified car ad.

LETI: I wrote that ad honestly.

PEARL: O K.

LETI: How else were we supposed to meet?

PEARL: How many girls did you interview before I came?

LETI: Twelve.

PEARL: I wasn't the first.

LETI: You'll always be.

PEARL: *(Glances at her watch)* Freddy and his brother are about an hour away. I got to go.

LETI: Even if you drop me, I'm in your blood.

PEARL: *(In jest)* Are you a vampire?

LETI: I won⬛t take you back.

PEARL: That's the last of my worries, Leti.

LETI: You were real easy about coming to Baja.

PEARL: That's right.

LETI: Easy about the arrangement with Freddy.

PEARL: So? What's your point?

LETI: There's a murderer inside you.

PEARL: If you think so. But I didn't kill anyone.

LETI: Are you setting me up?

PEARL: Why bother?

LETI: Blackmail.

PEARL: No

LETI: Just say the truth. What's in my skull?

PEARL: Did you think we were going to spend a long vacation together?

LETI: Yes.

PEARL: That's why you gave me the cash?

LETI: It's only money. That's my openness. *(Pause)* You think there's more cash stashed away. And you were going to swipe the rest in Rosarito.

PEARL: I don't steal.

LETI: Maybe there's another word for it?

PEARL: Gift giving.

LETI: My heart.

PEARL: I see your heart.

LETI: Where's the cash? *(Flip)* Stashed with Consuela in the salon?

PEARL: Doesn't she have an amazing hair lip for a salon owner?

LETI: Something bugged you last night.

PEARL: It was your garish nightgown.

LETI: Are you sure it wasn't the kiss?

PEARL: The cop's not tracking a homicide, he's just really interested in the drugs. I walked with him back into the hotel lobby. He wasn't going to mess with me 'cause it was all about you, Leti.

LETI: He could have busted you as an accessory.

PEARL: Given the circumstances, I was nice to him.

LETI: Either you're totally full of shit or you're very very lucky.

PEARL: I'm lucky. Like I said.

LETI: Why the hell would he let you go?

PEARL: My smile. I convinced him. *(Pause)* O K. I hugged him. *(Pause)* O K. I kissed him.

(Silence. A "Lolita smile". LETI gets it.)

LETI: And what about Freddy?

PEARL: Freddy? I wouldn't dream of taking him with me on a vacation. The older I get, the more I believe in my independence. *(Pause)* You don't look good.

LETI: That's how I am in the morning.

PEARL: Maybe we can't do anything else for each other. Nature can fail too.I don't know what else to say.

LETI: *"Lo siento, lo siento. Que lastima."* *(Pause)* I had a beautiful retriever two years ago.

PEARL: You told me that story.

LETI: The loveliest pet in the world. He never left my side. I might have died from loneliness without him. *(Pause)* You're very cruel, Pearl.

PEARL: Maybe.

LETI: You're now more insincere than me. You must want to see me ruined.

PEARL: No.

LETI: Because I wanted you, I became...

PEARL: We're all a little stupid when we light a candle and uncork some wine.

LETI: Yeah.

PEARL: Do you expect me to be a something I'm not?

LETI: No.

PEARL: Good. I'm not a golden retriever, Leti.

LETI: I never said you were.

PEARL: You knew I would take a few risks. Maybe you taught me an important lesson.

LETI: About what?

PEARL: About...

LETI: Give me another chance then.

PEARL: Part of me wants to.

(LETI touches PEARL's hair. PEARL lets her.)

LETI: Let's have breakfast.

PEARL: I don't want breakfast.

LETI: Let's have a long walk on the beach.

PEARL: *(Half a laugh. picking up LETI's Mexican shawl)* You can't follow me. And you can't run away.

LETI: I don't intend to run.

PEARL: And you can't stay here.

LETI: I know.

PEARL: Time's run out. I'm all different.

LETI: All right. I won't push. Give me a hug and just go.

(Slowly LETI and PEARL come together and hug. the next moment, PEARL breaks away.)

PEARL: Look outside the window.

LETI: Fred and his brother?

PEARL: Nope. The Mexican cop called for a back-up car.

LETI: *(Looks outside)* What are they waiting for?

PEARL: You.

LETI: Then why don't they just come up?

PEARL: Time to finish their coffee and cigars. You're small fry. Baja small fry.

LETI: No, you got it wrong, Pearl. It's Baja. They're small fry.

PEARL: *(Sincere)* The resort's gated and fenced along the ocean. There's only two ways outside and they know it.
   We've seen each other, Leti. There's nothing more. I keep hearing that "Pony Car, Pony Car" inside my head. *(Distracted)* I wanted something more.

(LETI and PEARL kiss. Awkward separation)

PEARL: I don't know what the hell I want.

LETI: Hand me my cigarettes... *(Not unkindly)* Get out.

PEARL: Better to bribe these cops for dope than risk getting discovered for murder. *(Pause)* Those two women in London who found shelter under a tree during a storm...just one deadly bolt of thunder.

LETI: One deadly bolt.

PEARL: Shouldn't one survive a storm? *(Pause)* I wish you I were more honest. *(Silence)* I'll always remember you fondly, Leti.

(PEARL exits. LETI waits a few seconds, puts an unlit cigarette in her mouth, goes to her bag, puts on glamorous dark glasses, gets a blonde wig and brushes it as lights fade, smiling, ready for a brazen getaway.)

END OF PLAY

www.ingramcontent.com/pod-product-compliance
Lightning Source LLC
Chambersburg PA
CBHW052221090426
42741CB00010B/2629